AquaGuide

Aquarium Plants

Dr Jürgen Schmidt

CONTENTS

Originally published in Germany in 1999 by bede-Verlag, Bühlfelderweg 12, D-94239 Ruhmannsfelden

First published in the UK in 2002 by Interpet Publishing, Vincent Lane, Dorking, Surrey RH4 3YX, UK

ISBN 1-84286-034-8

The recommendations in this book are given without any guarantees on the part of the author and publisher. If in doubt, seek the advice of a vet or aquatic specialist.

Translation: Heike de Ste. Croix

Unless otherwise credited, all photographs in this book are from M.-P. & C. Piednoir.

Beautiful tanks full of varied aquarium plants and fishes are the dream of every aquarist. Nevertheless, many budding waterplant enthusiasts soon give up their new hobby once their initial euphoria has abated, and they concentrate on other aspects of aquatics instead. In most cases the reason why they abandon this beautiful hobby is that the whole set-up of the tank is wrong. This book will chiefly focus on correct plant care and to start with we have to establish one important fact: if something is not quite right in the tank and the fishes are not happy, it very quickly shows in their behaviour; however, once you detect the first symptoms of disease in plants, any remedial care will generally come too late. It is a common misconception that plant care is much easier than fish care, as plants die much more slowly than animals.

However, provided that some basic rules are observed, plant care can be as easy – if not easier – as looking after fish, but without the

The combination of beautiful aquarium plants with attractive fishes is the aim of most aquarists. Unfortunately, only very few of them will concentrate on plants, although this aspect of aquatics is an extremely interesting hobby.

The so-called Amazon aquarium is almost a classic aquatic theme. Here you can see red neon and turquoise discus together with catfish. However, geographic origin was not a criterion when the aquatic plants were chosen – they include species from all over the world.

right water, nutrients and light, no plant will thrive. Just as fishes need to be fed daily, so plants also need basic nutrients and light daily. It goes without saying that light is as important to plants as food is to fishes. The fact that plants also need carbon dioxide just as fishes need oxygen is not commonly known or is often ignored. At night, when the lights are switched off, plants still breathe just like fish and for that they obviously need oxygen. However, in a well functioning aquarium plants often produce more oxygen through photosynthesis during the day than they actually need at night.

There are both tough and delicate plants now available and it is quite possible to keep some of the more robust species in poor light conditions.

This book will introduce you to hardy aquarium plants but it also includes the most popular of the more delicate and demanding species with their basic requirements for healthy growth.

Another well-known fact that is often quickly forgotten is that many of the plants available for aquariums are not real aquatic plants but bog plants which display various degrees of tolerance to being submerged under water. But even these plants can survive under water provided sufficient CO_2 and light is available. In order to avoid confusion this book will not distinguish between real aquatic plants and bog plants but simply talk about "water or aquarium plants".

In the early years of aquatics it was often assumed that certain aquarium plants could not be grown together. The fact is, however, that some species can compete successfully for

light and nutrients while others are not so successful. Provided both sufficient light and nutrients are available, the plants will not need to compete for survival and many different species can be grown together in an aquarium. Of course, you have to establish the right conditions with regard to water temperature, light intensity, water chemistry and such like. Alternatively, you can choose plants which can adapt easily to changing conditions in the aquarium.

Apart from observing the rules concerning the technical conditions of aquarium plant care, you should also be careful to select suitable plants to create a beautifully "green" aquarium.

Tasteful decoration and an attractive planting scheme are not the only criteria for an aesthetically pleasing aquarium. The positioning of the tank and its surroundings are just as important. No matter how much care you take with the interior decorations and planting scheme of your aquarium, the effect will look insignificant if the surround-ings are not right. So it is important to consider this aspect before setting up your aquarium as you will not be able to reposition it once it is fully functioning.

Geographical considerations played no role in the set-up of this aquarium. The visual effect of the combination of a variety of plants, decorations and fishes, guppies here, is the overriding factor.

You can create a beautiful aquarium filled with aquarium plants provided you observe the following precaution: don't just position your new aquarium in any old place, fill it with water, introduce some plants and then expect them to thrive. The completely opposite approach, i.e. careful planning, is the key to success.

Although aquarium plants require a lot of light, the aquarium should not be placed too close to a window as the effect of natural daylight cannot be controlled and subsequently will lead to algae growth. The best place for an aquarium is out of direct sunlight.

Don't buy a cheap aquarium. Buying a good quality product will reduce the likelihood of accidents caused by leaks.

Aquariums with silicone seals are just as good as tanks with a frame, which mostly just serves as a decorative border. Ideally the seals should be made of black silicone as algae or fungi cannot grow on them, a problem which would subsequently weaken the seal. If possible, always choose a large aquarium for aquarium plant cultivation. The larger the surface area, the easier it is to create a beautiful aquarium; the aquarist can develop his or her creativity and the plants will thrive.

7

Positioning the aquarium

This is a fundamental factor which plays an important role in the proper functioning of the aquarium. The situation should be chosen carefully for easy access and to show off the aquarium to its best advantage. Once the aquarium is fully installed, you cannot easily change its position as you will be unable to move a full tank. Therefore, never rush into deciding the right place for your aquarium nor in setting it up.

In general, the floor has to be strong enough to carry the weight of an aquarium that is filled with 300-400 litres (66-88gal) of water; any weight greater than this should be approved by a qualified architect.

Under no circumstances should you place an aquarium directly in front of or opposite a window or any other glass surface which lets in light. Daylight, and especially direct sunlight, inevitably leads to rapid growth of algae and light reflected in the glass

To show off such a beautiful community aquarium of plants and fishes to best effect, it has to be in the right place. It would be a shame if this attractive tank had to "compete" with a television set.

In contrast to a community aquarium, a beautiful species aquarium can also be very impressive. Here the dwarf ambulia, Limnophila sessiliflora, *dominates the tank together with the pearl gourami,* Trichogaster leerii *.*

will spoil the view of the aquarium.

The best place is therefore as far away from any window as possible. The area immediately above the aquarium should be completely clear to make daily maintenance easy. Tight corners or a spot under a staircase just cause a lot of problems.

But light is not the only factor to be considered when positioning your aquarium. The floor has to be absolutely level, which can be achieved by placing special sheets directly underneath the tank and, of course, it has to be strong enough to bear the weight of the aquarium.

Tip: You should leave sufficient room around the aquarium to be able to carry out daily maintenance comfortably.

The water supply should not be too far away from the aquarium so that you can carry out the necessary water changes easily. It is also sensible not to lay an expensive carpet below the tank.

The aquarium stand
While the type of material is

irrelevant, its capacity to bear weight is not. You can either buy a proper aquarium stand or an existing piece of furniture might be suitable provided it can carry the enormous weight **– the weight in kilos of a fully equipped aquarium is 50 per cent more than its water capacity in litres,** which means that a container filled with 100 litres (22gal) of water weighs 150kg (330lb). In addition the surface of the stand has to be the same size as the base of the aquarium tank. Ideally it should be slightly larger, but certainly never smaller. The surface has to be even and completely level, and this can easily be checked with a spirit level and, if necessary, adjusted. Then place a waterproof plywood board on the stand and on top of this position either a polystyrene or polyurethane board, which will even out any unevenness. The aquarium must never overlap this base!

The base can either be integrated into a piece of furniture or panelled as such. Aquariums with a capacity of more than 300 litres (66gal) are best placed on a base made of square metal supports with a diameter of 4-5cm (1.5-2in). The number of legs depends on the length of the aquarium; e.g. the base for a 2m (6ft) long tank should have at least six legs.

Fitting out your aquarium

The setting up of any aquarium should be done logically in stages. In order to get unspoilt pleasure from your aquarium, aesthetic considerations should not be overlooked. Always avoid siting your aquarium in dark and unwelcoming places; these are almost always corners. The style of the aquarium should match that of the room's interior. This is not always easy to achieve, but, for example, an aquarium with a modern stand does not look good in a room furnished with antiques.

The aquarium should be as far away as possible from the television so that one does not distract from the other. The bottom of the aquarium should ideally be 1 metre (3ft) above the floor, so that it is at eye level for a sitting adult or a standing child.

When choosing your first aquarium, go for a classic and simple style with just a frontal view. At this stage avoid choosing partition aquariums, i.e. tanks which are fixed to a wall and can be admired from three sides, built-in aquariums or those which are free-standing in the middle of the room. These tanks are for experts and it would be a shame if you lost interest in this beautiful hobby because you started off by being too ambitious.

Pennywort, Hydrocotyle, and platies, Xiphophorus – a successful combination. Specialization is a real art in aquatics; it means looking after a few species only.

Note: The aquarium must not stand in direct sunlight, which will cause rapid algae growth. Therefore, avoid placing your aquarium either in front of or opposite a south-facing window.

Make sure that you leave sufficient room to move around the aquarium for the initial set-up and the regular water changes. It makes sense to situate your aquarium near a drain, e.g. a toilet, sink, shower or bath.

To ensure you have easy access to the aquarium, position it a couple of centimetres away from a wall so that the lid can be easily lifted and removed. Ideally, work to a plan, consider all the options and draw up several designs before you decide on a place in the room.

Tip: The most important thing to remember is that everything is possible while the aquarium is still empty.

Apart from plants and fish, there is the water to be considered and once the aquarium is filled, it cannot easily be moved.

Cleaning and rinsing the aquarium
When cleaning the aquarium, always use a soft sponge and lukewarm water, without any detergent. During the final rinse check that the aquarium is level and that it has no

leaks. Unfortunately, leaks are not unusual nowadays in mass-produced tanks.

Designing the background

Plants, which are positioned in front of a backdrop of a wall covered with cables and pipes do not look good. Many aquarists therefore stick a background poster behind the back wall of the tank. Large selections of such posters, not all of them particularly tasteful though, are available from aquatic shops.

But there is another, more simple, solution: you can attach a piece of black cardboard or cork to the outside of the back wall of the aquarium.

Once this is done, you can place the aquarium in its chosen spot; remember to leave a couple of centimetres gap between its back wall and the wall of the room to accommodate cables and pipes.

Technical equipment

Equipment for aeration (which is not necessary for plant aquariums), filtration, heating and carbon dioxide release is usually fitted at the back of the tank where it can be easily

The simplest solution to covering the back wall of your aquarium is to fix black cardboard to the back of the tank and use tall-growing plants, here Vallisneria, *to cover most of the back-ground.*

hidden. Should you want to use an external filter, then these are available either partially or fully equipped with the filter materials. The heating element must not come into contact with plastic.

Note: Electrical equipment must never be switched on outside the water!

Decorating your aquarium

Decorations will give the aquarium its individual look and are ideal for concealing technical equipment behind them.

Contrary to popular belief, stones which have been thoroughly cleaned, and large pieces of bogwood should be arranged first before the substrate is filled in and levelled out.

Tip: Any unstable structures, which might collapse or fall over, should be avoided.

Silicone adhesive, the type which is also used to seal the aquarium walls, can also be used to glue several stones together. However, all surfaces to be joined must be completely dry and clean; any grease can be removed with acetone.

Should you wish to separate the stones at a later stage, this can be done easily with a sharp razor blade.

Tip: Do not use your aquarium as a display cabinet for a collection of stones. The best effect is achieved by using only one type of stone, slate for example.

Above all, don't let your imagination run wild, but try to create a natural-looking display with stones and wood.

Tip: It is advisable that you try out your decorations on "dry land", i.e. in front of the aquarium, until you are completely satisfied with your design.

This will limit the risk of falling structures scratching or possibly even cracking the tank walls.

Mangrove wood roots or bogwood will give the aquarium a natural look. The wood must, however, be thoroughly cleaned before it is positioned in the tank, either by scrubbing or better still by using a high-pressure hose. If you are looking for perfection, then immerse the timber completely in boiling water for several hours.

Even if you take all these precautions, you still cannot avoid the roots turning the water yellow or brown. This is caused by humic acids and tannins leaching out from the wood over several months. The regular water change will alleviate this effect but the discoloration of the water will take some of the natural light away from the plants. Basically this effect is quite harmless and sometimes even beneficial to many plants. The roots will make the water more acidic, which makes it ideal for plants whose natural habitat is of that type. Brown discoloration is actually ideal for an Amazonian aquarium.

Substrates

I recommend that you use medium grain quartz gravel in a layer approximately 10cm (4in) thick.

But there are also other types of suitable gravels available varying in quality and colour. River sand is mostly used for aquarium purposes because of its versatility. Sand from new red sandstone is very light and fine and is especially effective in tanks which hold dark-leafed plants like Cryptocorynes or some types of *Aponogeton* and *Nymphaea*.

Black gravel gives an aquarium depth and if planted up densely it can look quite luxurious. This substrate is best suited for really modern aquariums, for example those with a black frame or a convex front wall.

In addition, dark gravel hardly reflects any light and the plants will not be exposed to any unwanted radiation from below.

Don't be tempted to buy recycled gravel, which is often sold at special prices by wholesalers, as it may contain substances which could be harmful to plants and fish. Sea sand should also be avoided as it contains too much chalk, which makes it more suitable for sea- or brackish water tanks.

Once you are confident you have selected the right medium, put it in boiling water for a few minutes. Allow it to cool, add some fertilizer and spread a layer approximately 6cm (2.5in) deep on the aquarium floor. Then add a 10cm (4cm) layer of clean gravel at the front of the tank. The surface layer can gradually increase towards the back with a maximum thickness of 12-15cm (5-6in) at the back wall.

The bottom material

The substrate helps plants to root and contains nutrients. Each plant acquires its own space where it will root and absorb nutrients. The bottom of the tank is also where most of the nitrogen cycle takes place. Excrement from fish and food remains settle on the substrate

These courting lemon tetra, Hyphessobrycon pulchripinnis, *use the delicate* Hemianthus micranthemoides *as a spawning substrate. In the background grows a large* Alternanthera reineckii. *Both plant species need plenty of light. The* Alternanthera *is best placed in the centre of the aquarium and* Hemianthus micranthemoides *in the foreground, but it can also be planted around the edges because of its garland-like leaves.*

15

The aquarium for water plants

Bog plants like this Crypto-coryne beckettii *in the foreground need a mineral-rich substrate. However, you must never use ordinary plant fertilizers for your aquatic plants as they contain substances that are harmful to fish.*

where bacteria turn them into mineral salts with the help of oxygen, which are then absorbed by the plants.

> **The activity of micro-organisms provides the substrate with more or less all the nutrients which are beneficial to the plants.**

The bottom material makes it possible for plants to root and provides nutrient salts. Roots must be able to penetrate its structure. This makes substrates with a very fine grain unsuitable as it will stick after some time. Quartz gravel is the traditional bottom for any aquarium; it is stocked by most aquarium shops and is suitable for many plants. However, you have to bear in mind that it does not contain many nutrients, which are only added after the aquarium has been fully stocked with plants and fish and once the nitrogen cycle has started. Even then the substrate may still be lacking certain nutrients, which can be added at a later stage.

Water

Water is obviously an element without which an aquarium plant cannot survive. Some fish and plants however prefer soft acidic water (e.g. *Vallisneria*, certain types of *Cryptocoryne*, *Echinodorus*, *Anubias*), whereas others need hard basic water (e.g. *Myriophyllum*) and others still have no preferences (e.g. *Ceratophyllum*, *Ceratopteris*).

For a plant to thrive it is logical that you should re-create the conditions of its natural habitat.

It is therefore essential that you enquire about their origins and cultivation requirements before you decide which plants to buy.

The right water

The quality of the water has to match the requirements of the chosen plants. If you only use tap water, which varies in quality and hardness depending on the area where you live, then you have to accept that not every plant can adjust to these conditions as most tap water is too soft.

Aquatic plants with red leaves need plenty of light, a good fertilizer, sufficient CO_2 fertilization and, last but not least, superb water quality.

17

Another important aspect is the cleanness of the water. Only the absence of particles in suspension allows sufficient light to reach the bottom of the tank. If the water is clear, all leaves and even the stems of the plants can get sufficient light.

Filling the aquarium with water

Two methods have been tried and tested. The first one is to use a hosepipe which leads directly from a tap to the aquarium. However, this is not always popular with the lady of the house as the pipe can come off the tap (a clip can help to secure it) or slide out of the tank (ensure that you fix it properly to the aquarium). Buckets can be used instead to fill the tank, but even this can be hazardous for carpets or parquet flooring. Both methods also have the disadvantage that the pressure of the water can disturb the interior set-up. In order to avoid disturbance to the substrate, place a bowl or a plate into the aquarium, let the water run into it and then spill over into the tank. In this way,

neither the gravel nor the fertilizer in it will be disturbed.

Only fill the tank to 20cm (8in) below the maximum water mark as this allows you still to make final adjustments to technical equipment and interior design at this stage. To do this you have to put your hand and arms into the water – and what would happen if the aquarium was filled to the limit? It would spill over!

At this stage you will notice that the aquarium looks a lot smaller than the empty tank did – by about a third to be precise. This is completely normal and is caused by the refraction of light in the water. If necessary you can still change the position of some of the equipment at this stage.

The first checks

First turn the heating on and set it at 24°C (75°F), then turn the filter on, followed by the air supply – and then...relax for a while. Ideally carry out these tasks over a whole day; admittedly this is not a lot of work. The next day will be dedicated to testing. The water should have settled and become clear by then and the water temperature should have reached around 24°C (75°F); now is the time to carry out minor adjustments. You have slept on your

Especially demanding species like this onion plant, Crinum thaianum, *need clean water, but water hardness is not important in the care of this plant. The onion plant needs a soil which is rich in nutrients. In water heated to a temperature of 24°C (75°F), this plant, which loves water movement, requires minimum care in a mixed plant tank.*

The aquarium for water plants

Once the tank is set up and planted, it requires a long time and a lot of patience before a beautiful Dutch aquarium such as this will grow to maturity.

first impressions overnight and it is still possible to change things.

> **The water level should not be changed at this stage as the plants have still to be introduced.**

If you are impatient now and absolutely have to do something to the aquarium, you can test the water chemistry by either using instruments specifically designed for this purpose or liquid testing kits, which are available from every aquatic shop.

The set-up and interior design of the aquarium is not really that difficult and most people can cope with it. You may be happy with the result but the aquarium still looks boring without plants and fishes. Be patient – you can start planting soon. But remember fishes cannot be introduced for at least another two weeks – only very few aquarists keep exclusively plant aquariums. Experienced aquarists will tell you – and they are quite right – that the water is "fresh" and has to "settle down", which means some biological and chemical processes have to get going and stabilize

Open tanks have the advantage that light can fall straight onto the water and is not diffused or filtered through a lid. However, you cannot keep jumping fish in this type of aquarium.

before fishes should be introduced.

Aquarium plants in a community tank

The aquarium is filled with water and now you want to introduce plants and fishes...

A community tank should accommodate fishes and a variety of plant species. It is therefore important to establish which species of plants and fishes can live happily together. As a basic rule fishes should be introduced roughly two weeks after the planting has finished. The reason for this is that to begin with large amounts of nitrite are released and these are only broken down once the bacteria population has increased and the nitrogen cycle has started. Once this has got under way the fishes can move in.

Plants are an integral element of and contribute to a balanced overall impression of the aquarium. Plants containing chlorophyll absorb carbon dioxide (in gaseous form) and with the aid of light convert it to oxygen, a process which is known as photosynthesis. However, they also absorb nitrites, nitrogen compounds which are created by the breakdown of organic substances, such as fish excrement and the remains of uneaten food.

The aquarium for water plants

Once the initial planting is finished, there is still space between these Cryptocorynes seen in the foreground. In order that these areas do not get covered with algae, you can either introduce catfishes or fast-growing plants, which can later be removed once the Cryptocorynes have spread.

In nature plants allow adult and young fishes to hide and lay eggs. And, last but not least, they provide food for herbivorous species, which means some of them will be destroyed but this need not damage the overall effect.

Tip: Introduce algae-eating shrimps and fishes to your waterplant aquarium.

Some waterplant aquariums are an exception to this rule and you can introduce fishes a few days after

animals (shrimps and snails) into the tank.

Real or artificial plants?

Of course, this book is not about artificial aquarium plants, which should only be used in tanks stocked with plant-eating fishes. But a large part of the aquarium vegetation consists not of aquatic plants but of bog plants. In their natural habitat, parts of these plants remain above the water level. Often after heavy rainfall they will get submerged under water but very rarely are they totally submerged all year round. They develop different leaves for air and water respiration, a fact which often comes as a surprise to aquarists.

All of these more or less amphibious plants are easily recognized by their stiff leaves, which only appear above the water level. They are comparatively soft and cannot survive out of water; the lack of supporting tissue makes them fragile and the stems snap easily. In general their leaves are more finely feathered than those of marsh plants. Plants need minerals, which should be introduced during the set-up of the aquarium. Solid fertilizers can be mixed with the bottom material where they are eventually broken down. Liquid fertilizer can simply be

finishing planting. One condition to observe, however, is that water temperature and chemistry are stable and appropriate for the new arrivals. To avoid algae growth during the first weeks put algae-eating fishes or other

In this aquarium both the brightness of the lighting and the choice of plants and fishes are correct; while the selection is not governed by geographic region of origin, every-thing is in harmony.

added to the water. Both types are available from aquatic shops – you must never overdose as this would "burn" the plants. The right dosage will ensure healthy growth and improve the plants' resistance to diseases.

Note: The importance of lighting is often underestimated and this will have a noticeable effect on plant growth.

As a rule of thumb use 1 watt per three litres (5 pints) of water volume for weak lighting and 1 watt per two litres (3 pints) of water volume for "normal" lighting. But:

Some aquarium plants are more demanding and require 1 watt per litre (1.75 pints) of water.

Therefore, an aquarium containing 100 litres (22gal) of water should be equipped with at least two fluorescent lighting tubes. A combination of two different types of lamp, "daylight" and "light optimized for plant growth" which have complementary spectral characteristics, is ideal. This weak lighting, however, is not sufficient for some of the more demanding aquarium plants.

Another alternative is to use mercury vapour lamps.

Lighting

The most important factor in guaranteeing successful aquarium plant care will be discussed now. The old formula states that 1 watt of light should be sufficient for two or three litres of water. The use of this simple formula is only safe in exceptional circumstances, e.g. for very shallow tanks or very robust plants, for example Java moss *Vesicularia dubyana*, *Anubias* (arum family) or *Cryptocoryne*. For demanding plants in an aquarium with a normal water depth of 50cm (20in) above the bottom, you should work with a ratio of at least 1:1, i.e. 1 watt of light per litre of water.

This means that a 300-litre (66gal) aquarium would have to be fitted with five 60 watt fluorescent tubes.

For larger aquariums the use of mercury vapour lamps has proved to be successful as these emit a lot of light. They light up the aquarium in a circular pattern, but this it is not as critical for tanks with a large surface area as it is for tanks with a small one.

Note: A day in the tropics has approximately 12 hours of daylight. Therefore the aquarium must not be lit for longer than 13 hours.

Longer periods of lighting will simply encourage the growth of algae. As the plants are used to a regular pattern of day and night, it would be sensible to install a time clock to control the lighting.

In general stem plants grow quickly and root easily. They are usually sold in clumps and are not potted up. Amongst this group of plants you will find popular genera such as *Myriophyllum*, *Cabomba* and *Limnophila*. If planted in groups they must have strong lighting. Their leaves are finely feathered which give the aquarium an aesthetically appealing look.

The plants of the *Ludwigia* and

Aquatic plants with fine or red leaves need plenty of light. This is very noticeable when you compare differently coloured varieties, such as the Myriophyllum seen in this picture. These species are the fastest-growing aquatic plants.

Hygrophila groups have stiff leaves which are not as finely feathered and

25

they make a fine contrast to the previously mentioned varieties. Other fast-growing plants are those with wide or narrow ribbon-type leaves, which grow directly out of the planted root. They belong to the *Sagittaria* and *Vallisneria* genera, and *Vallisneria americana* and *V. spiralis*, especially grow quickly towards the light until they have reached the surface of the water. Vallisneria propagate by producing side shoots, which spread horizontally from the stem and the runners produce new plants.

For the middle and foreground of the aquarium low-growing plants such as *Cryptocoryne* and *Echinodorus* (*Echinodorus tenellus* or *E. quadricostatus*) are suitable. They need relatively little light and grow slowly. Under perfect conditions they form a beautiful carpet. *Ceratophyllum demersum*, a European plant, easily adapts to tropical aquariums. It even thrives without being properly planted. Simply wedge the stems between two stones or leave them to float on the water surface where they can benefit from the light. Brittle stems can be used as cuttings for propagation.

Amongst the floating plants the Oriental water fern, *Ceratopteris*, is the most interesting; it propagates by producing new shoots on the margins of the leaves. It also grows quickly in any substrate.

The crystalwort, *Riccia fluitans*, grows more or less into a thick carpet on the surface. To keep the plant under control it is necessary to remove parts of it on a regular basis. As with other plants of this type, it covers any submerged plants and prevents them from flourishing.

Vesicularia dubyana, Java moss, covers the surfaces of stones, wood and sometimes even the walls of the aquarium. It grows relatively slowly but given time it creates a beautiful effect. It is a superb spawning substrate for many fish.

The majority of all these plants are sold in most aquatic shops; only *Ceratophyllum*, *Riccia*, Oriental water fern and Java moss are not always readily available.

The crystalwort, Riccia fluitans, is a floating plant which is prone to algae infestation.

The Indian fern, Ceratopteris thalictroides, can either be planted into the substrate or simply let float on the water surface, which is its natural habit. The Indian fern is a very robust plant; it can survive with very little light. The very fine underwater leaves of this floating fern are often mistaken for roots. The Indian fern is pictured here with the ever popular cardinal tetras, Paracheirodon axelrodi.

The aquarium for water plants

Java fern, Microsorium pteropus, and a variety of Cryptocoryne have been planted in this South-east Asian aquarium. These fishes are Penang betta, Betta pugnax, a mouth-brooding fighting fish, and dwarf gourami, Colisa lalia.

Tip: It is not essential to transport aquarium plants in water. They will not come to any harm if wrapped in wet newspaper.

Fragile species should be carried in plastic bags, which are also used for transporting fishes.

Light

Light is essential for photosynthesis as the process of energy production is dependent on its use of light. The photons, i.e. the invisible particles or waves which make up light, fall onto the green pigments of the leaves, chlorophyll, which subsequently causes a chemical reaction. The elements iron and hydrogen derived from water molecules also play a part in this process.

The best illumination for plants is sunlight. It provides the full spectrum of radiation from ultraviolet through blue, green, yellow, and red to infrared; parts of this spectrum can be seen as a rainbow. Every visible colour is principally a reflection of a certain area or wavelength of the spectrum, while the other colours are absorbed.

> The green pigments in plants show that only blue and red wavelengths are absorbed from the visible spectrum, while the green wavelength is reflected.

This is also the reason why only fluorescent lighting tubes are used in aquarium plant care as they emit a lot of the absorbable colours, which are visible to the human eye as pink.

If light is indispensable to plants, so is darkness, otherwise a constant production of sugar in the plant would result in leggy growth. Therefore, every aquarist must provide his or her plants with a constant cycle of light and darkness. Even in the tropics daylight lasts little more than 12 hours.

Photosynthesis

The majority of animals derive their energy from the synthesis of lipids (fats) and carbohydrates (simple and complex sugars). Carbon (one of the building blocks of fats and carbohydrates) and nitrogen (a major component of edible proteins) are the elements which the organism uses to build and rebuild its body. Any living creature, be it a plant or an animal, has to obtain nutrients in order to be able to produce energy, to grow and to reproduce.

Green plants, however, are not all the same. The energy required for their functioning comes from a combination of sunlight, carbon (C) from carbon dioxide gas (CO_2) in the atmosphere, and nitrogen (N) from their environment. This energy synthesis is called photosynthesis, a phenomenon that can only happen in daylight or under artificial lighting.

Water absorbed by plants plays an important role in the chemical reaction of photosynthesis and produces oxygen (O). Carbon dioxide gas, dissolved in water (H_2O), and mineral salts are converted into glycosides (sugar compounds) by the plant. This is mainly glucose ($C_6H_{12}O_6$), a simple molecule which can easily combine with the long molecular chain of cellulose. Cellulose is the basic building block for plant fibres, which give the plant a certain stability. Glucose is processed into starch, which is stored as reserves for the plant, and other sugar compounds, which form the plants' sap. Photosynthesis is the totality of a chain of chemical reactions. Iron and manganese are also essential for its functioning.

Photosynthesis begins as soon as light hits the green parts of plants, i.e. in those places where the pigment chlorophyll is present. But

Aquariums lit with spot lights, e.g. mercury vapour lamps, have lighter and darker areas, which gives them a natural appearance of partially shaded water.

like any other living creature, plants also absorb oxygen and give off carbon dioxide. During daylight oxygen production from photosynthesis is greater than the plant's oxygen consumption, but at night the plant only gives off carbon dioxide.

Selecting the right lighting

Before the invention of fluorescent tubes (not "neon lights" as they are too frequently called), aquarium lighting was inadequate to allow plants to thrive. The quality and variety of fluorescent light tubes that are available today, however, will provide optimum lighting as long as the water level does not exceed 50cm (20in). The reason to keep the water to this maximum depth is that light is absorbed by the glass lid and the water itself; this effect is even more pronounced when the water is cloudy or coloured, for example in a South American aquarium with its typical black water, where no more than 20 per cent of the light reaches the floor of the tank!

Aquariums with a water depth of more than 50cm (20in) should be equipped with special lighting, e.g. metal halide lights, which are strong enough for the rays to penetrate to the bottom of the tank.

Mercury vapour lamps, however,

are more for the expert aquarist, who is very experienced in the care of large aquariums.

Among all the varieties of fluorescent lights available, those that resemble "plant light" are the most popular with aquarists. They provide the right amount of light for plants to flourish and even enhance the colour of fish. Their disadvantage is that they just don't look natural. But you can buy fluorescent lighting which imitates natural daylight. Daylight tubes are neutral in colour without any visible emphasis and make plants and fish look completely natural. An ideal combination would be daylight and "plant light" fluorescent tubes, either in equal quantity or with a higher proportion of daylight tubes.

But the quality of the lighting is not the only important factor for plants:

Note: The necessary amount of light required for good aquarium plant care is often underestimated.

This is often the case with aquariums that are sold as a complete package with lighting equipment. Under normal conditions you should allow one watt per two to three litres (0.4-0.6gal) of water.

In general I recommend that you illuminate your aquarium for between 12-13 hours a day. Plants need a lot of light during this period in order keep their glucose production going; to illuminate your aquarium for longer period would simply encourage algae growth.

Note: One common error is the belief that a longer period of lighting will compensate for insufficient numbers of fluorescent tubes in the tank – or the opposite, that the lighting period can be reduced by installing more fluorescent tubes.

In addition the lighting must run continuously throughout the day, which reflects the natural requirements of plants; anything else would have a detrimental effect on their growth.

Dosing with carbon dioxide

Normal water conditions in a tank will provide a sufficient quantity of carbon dioxide gas.

Lack of carbon dioxide can be caused by strong movement in the water which causes carbon dioxide to be released into the atmosphere, or if the aquarium is densely planted but sparsely populated (e.g. in a Dutch plant aquarium or a Japanese natural aquarium). In both cases the pH value can rise to 7.5 or even 8.0. The first situation can be remedied

Plants of the Limnophila genus with their fine pinnate or bipinnate leaves need good CO_2 fertilization. Without CO_2 fertilizer the stems will grow leggy and turn transparent until the lower part disintegrates quicker than the plant can grow.

water and thus supplies sufficient amounts for healthy plant growth.

Note: Lack of carbon dioxide, or more precisely carbon, will result in poor plant growth as the plants cannot produce sufficient quantities of glucose as a result.

Aquarium plants absorb carbon dioxide through their upper cell layer, whereas garden or bog plants absorb it through special openings in their leaves.

Most aquarium plants cannot survive without carbon dioxide fertilizer. CO_2 fertilizing devices are very convenient and are quite

The Java fern, Microsorum pteropus, is one of the few very robust aquatic plants that need no fertilizer and can survive with very little light.

by reducing the movement of the water as long as the fish do not suffer and the filtration is still effective. CO_2 fertilizers are available from aquatic shops, which can raise the level of carbon dioxide in the water. Ensure you always follow the instructions carefully.

CO_2 fertilizers

Like oxygen, carbon dioxide gas is an important constituent of the atmosphere. In addition living organisms expel carbon dioxide through breathing. It dissolves in

inexpensive, and there is no reason why you should not equip your aquarium with one.

> **Tip: It is advisable to buy a device with a night timeswitch, which saves CO_2 and prevents excessive amounts of carbon dioxide from building up in the water, which would make respiration more difficult for plants and fishes.**

Nowadays there are several systems in use to dissolve CO_2 in water.

The simplest and most outdated, because of the high waste, involves bubbling carbon dioxide through the mineral aragonite. This method only allows a small part to be dissolved, the rest simply bubbles out of the water unused.

A better method is to introduce carbon dioxide through a membrane. The membrane is like a thin skin with extremely fine pores through which the gases get into the water without any of the water permeating into the gas container, which should be sited well below the water. But even this method has some disadvantages.

The main problem is that the upper surface of the membrane gets covered with algae, which reduces its permeability considerably. In

Green cabomba, Cabomba caroliniana, is one of those species in which even the green forms need CO_2 fertilizer. The stems can survive for a while without fertilizer but gradually they become smaller and fragile.

addition other gases which are released into the water find their way into the CO_2 storage canister where they pollute and dilute the carbon dioxide which ultimately affects its solubility. It is then necessary to empty the gas container completely and refill it with clean CO_2.

The most popular system works by feeding small CO_2 bubbles through a long system of spiral tubes directly into the water. The gas bubbles move towards the surface and water is taken with them so that the water is constantly changed in the system and new water is loaded

33

Bacopa monnieri *belongs to a group of aquatic plants which can grow quite well without CO_2 fertilizer, but if fertilizer is used, the plants grow even better and are more compact.*

with CO_2. The bubbles move with the water upwards through the pipe and while the gas is being dissolved in the water the bubbles become smaller. Once the CO_2 supply has settled at an ideal level, the flow of bubbles is reduced to a rate at which it no longer reaches the water surface. This system is now available in a variety of technical designs from various companies.

The carbon dioxide is supplied in standard bottles which can be replaced. The expensive part of this system is the pressure-reduction valve, which must be adjustable to the tiniest amounts. It must also be equipped with a timer so that it can be turned off at night. The ideal equipment consists of a pH-meter which directly controls the CO_2 supply. This means setting the desired pH value to 6.8; if it falls below this figure the CO_2 supply is reduced or stopped, if it rises above this level, the CO_2 supply is increased. You need the right CO_2 content to create a balance with the dissolved carbon dioxide in the water, also known simply as carbonic acid, and this allows you to maintain a constant level of CO_2 in the water while also enabling you to keep the pH value stable during the day. For the system to work the water must not be too soft as even the smallest amounts of CO_2 would then change the pH value.

Fertilizing

Although CO_2 and mineral fertilizing are physiologically comparable processes for plants, they are treated separately in aquatics as they are technically different procedures. Real aquatic plants absorb all the essential minerals through their leaf surfaces. Aquatic plants either do not have any roots or they have simple root structures whose purpose is not the intake of nutrients but to anchor the plants in the base of the aquarium. Therefore pure aquatic plants are always fed with fertilizers that dissolve in water.

Real aquatic plants must be fed with water-soluble fertilizers.

It is different for bog plants. They grow partially above the water surface and have to absorb nutrients through their roots, just like any other plant.

Bog plants need fertilizers that are mixed with the soil.

Floating plants usually have their own category; they have some of the characteristics of aquatic and bog plants but in addition they have structures which are unique to their type. They root in the substrate and absorb most of the minerals from it.

Even floating plants need a good fertilizer in the bottom soil.

Solid fertilizers are mixed with the substrate during the set-up of the aquarium; some even look like large gravel particles. This gives satisfactory results but over the months the fertilizer dissolves, so it is quickly used and has to be replaced regularly. Obviously mixing new fertilizer with the bottom material is quite impractical. Certain products are designed so that they can simply be spread directly over the substrate surface. It is hardly surprising that solid fertilizers are replacing the liquid ones.

Another way to solve the problem is by mixing soil with sand. But this method requires a certain amount of experience. The common mix consists of 40 per cent pure sandy soil without any chemical fertilizer (be careful with soil of this type that is sold in garden centres!), 10 per cent clay and 50 per cent fine unwashed sand (river sand). This type of base is spread on the

Alternanthera reineckii can only be kept in an aquarium provided that the conditions with regard to light, fertilization and CO_2 provision are perfect. If kept under optimum conditions, the plant will even produce some flowers.

aquarium floor between two layers of gravel. At this stage you can no longer "dig around" in the base without disturbing the soil. Consequently this procedure is described as quite delicate.

Some clever aquarists put this soil mixture into plastic planting pots or even use yoghurt pots or the lower half of a plastic bottle for this purpose. The plants are then individually planted into these containers and the soil cannot spread.

The depth of the substrate has to be sufficient to allow roots to spread but without distorting the overall design of the aquarium or piling up the bottom material unnecessarily high. In general the depth should be between 8-10cm (3-4in) with a gradual slope down from the back to the front of the tank.

As described earlier, solid fertilizers can be mixed with the base material during the set-up of the aquarium, but they gradually dissolve and have to be replaced. This is why you should not ignore liquid fertilizers that are sold in most aquatic shops. These fertilizers are absorbed by the plant leaves, especially those of true aquatic plants. The movement of the water, however, spreads these fertilizers around the aquarium and subsequently they are also absorbed by the roots. These fertilizers have only a limited shelf life and should therefore be stored in a cool and dark place. Ensure that you observe the manufacturers' instructions closely so that you do not damage your plants.

Note: Too much fertilizer can "burn" the plants.

Therefore you must never use liquid and solid fertilizers at the same time (unless, of course, they are specifically formulated to work together).

Don't even think about using fertilizers designed for garden plants or houseplants – they are not correctly formulated to meet the requirements of aquatic plants.

If some readers have used such products, take this as warning! Liquid fertilizers for garden or houseplants contain nitrogen compounds, which can be harmful to fishes and speed up algae growth.

Mineral salts

This term covers a number of substances without which plants cannot survive. They are better known as fertilizers, similar to those used by gardeners for garden- and houseplants. These substances are not only numerous but come in various shapes and forms. The most important ones are without doubt nitrogen compounds in the form of nitrates (NO_3^{2-}), phosphorus (P), e.g. as phosphate (PO_4^{3-}), and potassium (K). But other elements are also essential even though they are only present in very small amounts, and they are, therefore, known as trace elements.

Amongst these is iron (Fe), which plays an important part in the chemical reaction of photosynthesis. Magnesium (Mg) is equally important, as it forms the core of each chlorophyll molecule – no magnesium, no chlorophyll, no photosynthesis.

Note: Lack of iron and magnesium will create a chlorosis, a deficiency disease which causes leaves to turn yellow and the plant will start to wilt.

Elements like manganese (Mn), zinc (Zn) and copper (Cu) are also essential for healthy plant growth. These substances have to be present as ions dissolved in water (Mn^{2+}, Zn^{2+}, Cu^{2+}) so that they can be absorbed by the plants.

Vitamins

Another group of substances is also vital. Everyone knows how important vitamins are to our own health but their importance for plants is often neglected or ignored. Vitamin B_1 and B_{12} are especially important. To avoid having to delve too deep into chemical formulae, suffice it to say that a vitamin deficiency has a detrimental effect on plant growth and reproduction, even though it may not be visible to the naked eye.

Mineral salts are absorbed through the roots of aquarium plants; real aquatic plants absorb these substances also through their leaves.

Planting your new plants

It requires a lot of thought to create a beautifully planted aquarium. When you are planning the planting scheme, bear in mind that the small foreground plants grow in shallow water in their natural habitat and therefore require a lot of light.

The plants most commonly grown in aquariums generally come from the tropics and Europe. They are bred in greenhouses in conditions of extremely high humidity where they all grow above water. Each species has its own special water requirements (acidic and soft or alkaline and hard), so it pays to do some research on their preferences and how they can be grouped with other plants. Many of them can adapt to most conditions; they are quite robust and can thrive even in adverse conditions. One variety of plant will grow very tall, others are dwarf plants; some grow quickly, others slowly – it is up to the aquarist to choose. To make the right choice you should consider a number of points, but don't concentrate on it to such an extent that in your efforts to care for your plants, you forget about the fishes.

The cost of plants is a secondary concern as nowadays there are plants available to match everyone's purse. So it is worthwhile experimenting – you will surely find something suitable.

Plants need light, carbon dioxide and various mineral salts in different quantities. If even one of these elements is not present or a deficiency exists, it is no good simply increasing the supply of one or all of the other substances. Healthy growth of any plant depends on the presence of all these substances – this is essential for the correct living conditions.

Plants are not only important for decorative purposes in the aquarium. They contribute to balanced environmental conditions by producing oxygen, absorbing carbon dioxide and providing protection and a spawning ground for fishes. This is reason enough to provide the best possible conditions for their cultivation and to pay as much attention to their requirements as you would to those of the fishes.

> **Note: The majority of aquarium plants come from the tropics where temperatures range between 20° to 22°C (68-72°F) throughout most of the year.**

Only a few of them (*Cabomba, Myriophyllum*) live permanently under water and their leaves are very finely feathered and light in colour. These are delicate plants; they don't grow above the water surface and can break easily. The vast majority of aquarium plants are not really aquatic plants but bog plants (*Cryptocoryne, Hygrophila*). During the dry season you will find them either partially or completely out of the water in their natural habitat and their leaves are large and dark-green. Only during the rainy season are they submerged and their leaves are more delicate. This is how aquarists prefer them for aquariums and in this respect their life cycle is changed.

But there are more than just these two categories. There are floating plants, which develop root-like leaf structures but which do not root in the substrate. And there are the mosses and water ferns, which attach themselves to stones and roots.

Compared to freshwater varieties, only very few flowering plants can live in sea water. This is where algae are the dominant type; their simple structure which dispenses with stem and roots makes it possible for them to survive in the most hostile conditions, such as low tide, when they are completely out of the water and exposed to the sun. Some species (especially *Caulerpa*) adapt easily to the conditions of a marine aquarium.

> **Almost all aquarium plants available today are not gathered from their natural habitat but are cultivated in special nurseries in Europe and especially Asia.**

Bog plants are cultivated out of water in tropical conditions, i.e. hot

Planting your new plants

Only fill the aquarium to two-thirds of its capacity before you start planting. This way you avoid water spilling over while working in the tank. When position-ing the plants, make a small hole in the substrate, put the plant in it and firm the gravel back around the plant. The roots should, however, be trimmed back to 3-4cm (1-1.5in) and not be kept as long as shown in this picture.

with humidity near to saturation point and in well-soaked soil. Only true aquatic plants are cultivated under water.

The diversity of the plant kingdom can make it sometimes difficult for aquarists to come to terms completely with the subject and this applies mainly to plant nomenclature, which unfortunately every now and then forces us aquarists to cope with name changes. Unfortunately, some English common names and some scientific ones – which are quite difficult to remember – can be subject to change. Similar-looking plants are often mixed up and some plants are actually hybrids, which means a cross-breed between related species.

The art of planting

Planting is not really difficult, but never rush it – it should be done with great care once the initial water level has gone down a bit. Your aim is to arrange all the plants in the shape of an "amphitheatre", which means putting the large specimens at the sides and at the back of the tank, medium-sized plants are planted in the middle and the smallest ones at the front. This will create an impression of perspective when the aquarium is viewed from the front. Plants of the same species should be planted in groups but not too close together, so healthy growth is not hindered and sufficient light is able to get to all the plants. Stem plants, each of which develops in small bundles, should be planted approximately 4-5cm (1.5-2in) apart. This will allow sufficient room for their roots to spread. They must not be planted too deep either.

> **Tip: Only the bottom part of the plant, which is also often lighter in colour than the rest, should be planted into the substrate.**

All these jobs are done by hand and you can use your fingers as a dibber, but most aquatic shops sell tools which are specifically designed for planting. Finally, it should be observed that plants do not necessarily grow as you would want them to, but they will always grow towards the light.

The lighting will simulate the change from day to night, and a typical period of 13 hours of light is ideal for plants. You should always expect the colour of the leaves and the shape of the plants to change gradually as they adjust to the conditions in your aquarium.

Planting

The arrangement of plants in your aquarium is usually done both to satisfy your own aesthetic views and

Planting your new plants

Stem plants can be propagated by cuttings, as shown here on this water wisteria, Hygrophila difformis. The shorter young cutting is then planted in front of the old plant, as this will have lost most of its lower leaves.

also to recreate the plants' natural habitat. But you must never overlook certain technical aspects – for instance, there must be room for roots to develop and space for light to reach all the plants. Consequently plants must not be planted too close together nor too close to the aquarium walls, as roots must be able to spread horizontally and vertically. The light must be able to reach all leaves – even the lowest – without being blocked by the upper leaves.

Quite often you may see a well-established aquarium with dense plant growth but the lower stems are bare – this is not an attractive sight.

If, once all plants have been positioned, your aquarium still looks a bit sparse, just remember that the plants will spread depending on how much room is available for their subsequent growth.

Stem plants (e.g. *Cabomba*, *Hygrophila*, *Limnophila*, *Myriophyllum*) are planted approx. 2cm (0.8in) deep into the substrate, i.e. to just below the first set of leaves. Don't worry if these plants don't have any roots or perhaps just a few; they are cuttings, which have been taken from the top of an adult plant. Plants root very quickly in an aquarium; you don't need any artificial lighting during the first 48 hours as this helps promote root growth.

Rosette plants (e.g. *Echinodorus*, *Cryptocoryne*, *Vallisneria*) must not be planted too deep. Only the roots and a small part of the unpigmented plant base should be buried in the substrate. Tall-growing plants like *Anubias*, *Bolbitis* or Java moss need no planting, they are secured to hard elements like porous stones or roots.

Problems

It can sometimes happen that only a couple of weeks after planting some of your plants are thriving while others start losing their leaves. This problem happens all the time. One possible reason could be that the affected plants may have been raised out of water, and you now expect them to grow under water, which leaves them two alternatives. They either adjust to the conditions under water and replace their submersed foliage with leaves which are better suited to life under water and they suddenly come back to life with new leaves. Or the plants cannot adjust to being submerged in water or to the water conditions. You will have to accept this fact and look for other species to replace them.

Another common problem is that the plants survive, remain more or less green but do not grow at all. There could be various causes: the plants cannot adjust to the water conditions (problems with pH value or the hardness of the water), lack of mineral salts or carbon dioxide, or something completely different.

Iron deficiency

Sometimes you may notice yellowing of the plant, which is a typical sign of iron deficiency. In such cases you cannot simply drop a piece of iron into the tank and wait for it to rust. Plants cannot assimilate iron in this form (or at least only in minute quantities). Adding a liquid or solid fertilizer is much more effective, one which provides iron as well as other

If you keep fishes in your aquarium that tend to forage through the substrate, it is advisable to protect the plant roots with rocks. The plant shown in this picture is Cryptocoryne beckettii.

substances which are easily absorbed by the plants.

If, despite all this, plants still turn brown, develop holes in their leaves or even begin to rot, then it is usually the lighting which is at fault – it is either lacking in quality or quantity.

To become a good waterplant gardener you should always observe the following recommendations. They are mainly intended for beginners or for those people who have given up all hope of creating beautiful vegetation in their aquarium. Firstly, it is always advisable to go for the classic, robust and healthy growing plants. Sad-

Planting your new plants

In order to create a tastefully decorated aquarium avoid mixing too many plant species and different types of stones as this will spoil the overall impression for any onlooker.

looking plants are always a big disappointment to every aquarist.

And to avoid that disappointment you must provide a lightly fertilized substrate and replenish it at periodic intervals with a good quality liquid fertilizer. The actual planting of a plant is the first step to its successful cultivation as the position chosen for it will determine whether or not it flourishes in the future.

Plants will grow quite quickly under ideal conditions, especially stem plants. So you can content yourself with the realization that as a future aquarium plant grower, you will not only enjoy looking after your plants but you will also be able to propagate them.

Tip: The water in the aquarium must move in order to avoid a carbon dioxide "jam". At the same time, the motion must not be too agitated to avoid causing damage to fragile plants.

This chapter is dedicated to the most common and robust aquatic, bog and floating plants. A few of the more demanding species are also included; they have been chosen because they are attractive plants and are widely available.

The descriptions of their care and required water conditions have been kept brief deliberately as this aspect has already been covered in previous chapters. This chapter on species is designed to help you select plants which tolerate the same conditions and which can be grouped together in an aquarium, and also to help you to distinguish between good and less suitable aquarium plants.

Any special requirements of a particular plant which differ from the generally applicable rules are listed under "Special Features". Any peculiarities or special characteristics are also listed there. Old names or those that are no longer used, synonyms or frequent incorrect spellings are only mentioned if they are still being used in popular literature or may be encountered in some aquatic shops.

Distinction will only be drawn between true aquatic plants and bog plants if it is relevant to their care. This means that some of the bog plants at times may have to be cultivated outside an aquarium. If certain species need a rest period (either in dry or wet conditions), this is also mentioned where appropriate.

The Japanese rush, Acorus gramineus, *is actually not an aquatic plant as it cannot survive growing underwater. If planted on the edge of a garden pond, the Japanese rush will only survive the winter if protected from frost.*

Acorus gramineus
SOLANDER (1789)
Japanese rush

This bog plant is one of those varieties that cannot be kept totally submerged all the time. Even with optimum lighting and fertilization, it would die after a while.

Range: East Asia.

Fertilizer: Strong substrate fertilizer, clay, dissolved carbon dioxide.

Propagation: In dry conditions as a bog plant by rootstock division.

Special features: A bog plant which is more suitable for a garden pond than an aquarium. As not many fish will eat this plant, it can sometimes be kept in an

aquarium with plant-eaters.
Water: 2-22°dH; 0-10°dCH; pH value 6-8; 16-25°C (61-77°F).

Alternanthera reineckii
BRIQUET (1899)

Variable species with several forms and colours. Varieties with leaves with green upper surfaces and red or brown under surfaces are more dominant than those with almost pure green foliage. This difficult bog plant can only be kept in an aquarium under optimum conditions.

The long stems grow towards the light, and if lighting is insufficient they develop long internodes (a segment of the stem between two nodes, each bearing a leaf or leaves), which make the plant fragile and less attractive.

Range: South America. With some colour varieties it is not known whether they grow like this in their natural habitat or if they have been cultivated.

Fertilizer: Good quality substrate fertilizer, liquid fertilizer and a good quality CO_2 fertilizer.

Propagation: By cuttings or – very labour-intensive – by seeds. It is easier to propagate the more robust garden plant than the aquatic plant. Unfortunately, most types sold in aquatic shops are raised as garden plants, which do not adjust well to underwater conditions.

Special features: Despite that fact that it is certainly a difficult and demanding aquatic plant, many aquarists want it for their aquariums because of its attractive colour. The different types available vary in their suitability as an aquatic plant. The variety with solid red leaves has adjusted especially well to cultivation under water.

Water: 2-15°dH; 2-5°dCH; pH value 6-7.2; 17-28°C (63-82°F).

This is a pink Alternanthera sessilis var. rubra. This plant cannot survive growing submerged; however, it is a suitable bog plant for terrariums.

Alternanthera sessilis
DeCandolle (1813)

This is an attractive plant and so it is often sold as an aquatic plant in aquatic shops, although it is not suited to being kept submerged all the time.

Range: The tropics.

Fertilizer: Strong substrate fertilizer plus liquid fertilizer for the water as well as a good CO_2 fertilizer.

Propagation: By cuttings.

Special features: A bog plant that is best suited for keeping in a paludarium, this plant cannot survive if kept totally submerged.

Water: 0-18°dH; 0-8°dCH; pH value 6-7.5; 14-28°C (57-82°F).

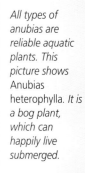

All types of anubias are reliable aquatic plants. This picture shows Anubias heterophylla. It is a bog plant, which can happily live submerged.

47

The dwarf anubias, Anubias barteri *var.* nana, is rarely found growing submerged in nature, but the plant adapts easily to aquarium conditions. The fresh flowers, however, will only appear if grown above water level.

Anubias barteri
SCHOTT (1860)

Anubias are robust aquatic plants. Even though they are bog plants, they can be kept submerged under water. The most popular and most common variety kept for aquatic purposes is *Anubias barteri* var. *nana*. This plant can be used for many purposes. It has to be planted densely if used at the front of the aquarium as it is quite slow-growing and it will take a while for all the gaps to be filled. If planted directly into the gravel, ensure that only the roots are in the substrate – the rhizome has to lie on top of it as it would rot if planted into the soil and this would subsequently lead to the decay of the plant. It is better to fix the plant to one of the tank decorations with a porous surface, for example a lava stone or a piece of bogwood. Its versatility makes this an ideal plant for all areas of the aquarium, especially if you want to hide the technical equipment in the tank. It also makes an attractive plant if allowed to grow outside the aquarium.

Range: West Africa.
Fertilizer: Liquid fertilizer.
Propagation: By rhizome division.
Special features: Anubias found in aquatic shops often have flowers which clearly indicate that the plants have been cultivated as bog plants on land.
Water: 0-27°dH; 0-12°dCH; pH value 5-8; 18-28°C (64-82°F).

The wavy-edged swordplant, Aponogeton crispus, is one of the types of swordplant least suited for aquatic purposes. This plant needs soft and acidic water; however, with sufficient CO_2 fertilization it can be kept in hard water. This robust species does not always need a period of dormancy, but when it is in hibernation the rhizome should be removed from the aquarium and stored in dark and slightly damp conditions.

Aponogeton longiplumulosus is a very attractive aquatic plant. During its dormant period it can remain in the aquarium. If the temperature during this period is kept as low as that of a cool room, the plant will be even more beautiful afterwards.

Aponogeton crispus
THUNBERG (1781)
Wavy-edged swordplant

This plant is the most robust of all *Aponogeton* species, which makes it an ideal aquatic plant. This species is available in different shapes and colours, varying from light to dark green and brown. While wild plants have long slender leaves, the cultivated varieties are more compact with shorter and broader leaves. Hybrids, plants that have been crossed with other species are also available.

As most Aponogetons experience regular periods of dormancy, it makes sense to grow them in containers. This makes it easier to move them from one tank to another when the need arises. The larger plants, whose leaves can grow easily to a size of 50cm (20in) or even longer, are only suitable for use in larger aquariums.

Range: South India and Ski Lanka.

Fertilizer: A good substrate and CO_2 fertilizer.

Propagation: By seed only.

Special features: The compact plants that are widely available nowadays are descendants from one single imported plant.

Aponogetons need a period of dormancy at cooler temperatures. Contrary to what was written in the past, this dormant period can take place in the aquarium. It is important to lower the temperature to between 10-20°C (50-68°F). The dormant period begins when the plant produces fewer leaves, which are also smaller than usual, and stops flowering.

Water: 0-17°dH; 0-8°dCH; pH value 5.5-7; 20-30°C (68-86°F).

Lately new colour varieties of Aponogeton longiplumulosus *have become available.*

Aponogeton longiplumulosus
VAN BRUGGEN (1968)

A good aquatic plant, which despite its dormant phase, can stay in the aquarium.
Range: Madagascar.
Fertilizer: A good substrate and CO_2 fertilizer.

Propagation: By seed.
Special features: see *A. crispus*.
Water: 2-20°dH; 2-8°dCH; pH value 6-7.5; 20-28°C (68-82°F).

51

The Madagascar laceplant, Aponogeton madagascariensis, is a very demanding plant.

Below: *Flowers of the Madagascar laceplant.*

Aponogeton madagascariensis
VAN BRUGGEN (1789)
Madagascar laceplant

This popular yet demanding plant needs cool water with strong movement and good filtration. As well as the large Madagascar laceplant, which grows taller than one metre (3ft), several smaller varieties are also widely known.

This species needs a dormant period, during which the plant can stay in the aquarium but the water temperature must be lowered during this time.

Range: Madagascar.

Fertilizer: Good substrate fertilizer, liquid fertilizer for the water and a good CO_2 fertilizer.

Propagation: By seed.

Special features: Because of its attractive leaves, this species is one of the most popular aquatic plants. Unfortunately, it is a delicate plant, which requires a lot of care. Sadly, most of the imported plants are taken from the wild, which could eventually make it an endangered species as the destruction of the tropical rainforests in its natural habitat is continuing on a large and threatening scale. Many aquatic shops now sell plants that are cultivated in nurseries.

Water: 0-10°dH; 0-4°dCH; pH value 5-7; 18-22°C (64-72°F).

Bacopa monnieri
PENNELL (1946)
Water hyssop

Bacopa monnieri does not grow particularly quickly, which makes it an ideal stem plant for group planting in the middle of an aquarium.

This plant does not have any special requirements with respect to water chemistry; it grows well in soft or hard water. However, it does not tolerate water pollution, and should this happen, then the plant sheds its lower leaves and the stems turn translucent and then rot. Lighting must not be too intense, medium lighting conditions are quite sufficient.

Range: The tropics and sub-tropical regions worldwide.
Fertilizer: Good substrate and CO_2 fertilizer.
Propagation: By cuttings.
Special features: Provided the individual stems are not planted too close together and they get enough light, all the leaves, even the lower ones, will last for a long time even when the stems are floating on the water surface.

Bacopa is also suitable for coldwater aquariums as it will tolerate moderate temperatures. It has to be overwintered indoors, however.
Water: 2-20°dH; 2-5°dCH; pH value 6-7.5; 16-30°C (61-86°F).

Bacopa monnieri *looks especially attractive if planted in groups. Plant short stems at the front and the longer ones at the back; this way you achieve the best visual effect.*

The African water fern, Bolbitis heudelotii, *is as attractive as it is demanding. If you consider aquatic plants just as an adjunct to a community aquarium, then do not include this plant in your tank.*

Bolbitis heudelotii
ALSTON (1934)
African water fern

The African water fern *Bolbitis heudelotii* is one of the more demanding aquatic plants. Its growing space must not be invaded by other plants; and fish excreta are more harmful still to this plant. The fern must not be planted directly into the substrate but rather should be tied to a piece of wood or a stone situated in the aquarium tank.

In its natural habitat in West Africa *Bolbitis heudelotii* grows exclusively in fast-moving water such as rapids, small streams and smaller fast-flowing rivers with sandy or rocky bottoms. The water flowing in these rivers is usually very clean, not very hard and has a slightly acidic pH value.

The plant's rhizomes cling to rocks and sandy beds but the roots never grow into the ground. The leaves stay mostly submerged but especially strong plants will push them all the way up to the surface of the water.

Range: West Africa.
Fertilizer: CO_2 fertilizer.
Propagation: By root cutting.
Special features: A very delicate plant that is hard to cultivate.
Water: 2-8°dH; 1-4°dCH; pH value 5-6.8; 22-28°C (72-82°F).

Cabomba caroliniana
GRAY (1837)
Green cabomba, Carolina fanwort
An ideal aquatic plant.
Range: South America, the Amazon, eastern USA, Carolina.
Fertilizer: Liquid fertilizer and a good CO_2 fertilizer.
Propagation: By cuttings.
Water: 2-20°dH; 0-6°dCH; pH value 6-7.5; 20-28°C (68-82°F).

Cabomba furcata
SCHULTES & SCHULTES
(1830)

Of the relatively undemanding fanworts, *Cabomba furcata* is the most demanding. Only soft and acidic water as well as strong lighting will guarantee long-term success in growing this plant. Neglecting the quality of the water just once can be fatal to the plant. A general rule in respect of care of *Cabomba* species is: the greater the proportion of red colouring in the leaves, the more difficult the plant is to look after. That is why the green *Cabomba caroliniana* is much better suited as an aquatic plant and why it is recommended for aquarists new to the hobby.
Range: The tropics of South and Central America.
Fertilizer: Liquid fertilizer and sufficient CO_2 fertilizer. Lack of fertilizer will cause the leaves to become translucent and decay.
Propagation: By cuttings, taken only from strong and healthy plants to avoid damage.
Special features: A delicate plant, only suitable for soft water aquariums.
Water: 0-8°dH; 0-3°dCH; pH value 5-6.5; 24-30°C (75-86°F).

In aquatic circles Cabomba furcata is better known under the synonym Cabomba piauhyensis. It is a very demanding and delicate plant, which needs soft water and plenty of light. Aquarists should choose Cabomba caroliniana instead.

Japanese cress, Cardamine lyrata, is an adaptable coldwater plant which also grows well in a tropical freshwater aquarium. However, good lighting is absolutely essential for healthy growth.

Cardamine lyrata
BUNGE (1835)
Japanese cress

This plant requires strong lighting conditions and should planted where there is slight water movement in the aquarium. In small aquariums with a water depth of up to 40cm (16in) *Cardamine lyrata* can be grown as a central plant. In larger aquariums it looks better if planted around the centre and as a transition to the planting scheme on the sides. This way it can develop easily into an attractive bushy plant. It also makes a beautiful contrast if planted next to species with dark green leaves.

Because of its rapid growth *Cardamine lyrata* is a good "filler" when setting up a new aquarium. This characteristic makes it very popular with impatient aquarists, who cannot wait until all the unattractive empty spaces have disappeared and who love to see evidence of new growth. But the rapid growth of *Cardamine lyrata* also has its disadvantage, as the plant can easily swamp a whole aquarium within weeks and drastic steps to reduce it have to be taken if it is not to run riot in the tank and crowd out other plants of a more delicate disposition.

Range: Eastern China, Eastern Siberia, Korea and Japan.
Fertilizer: Liquid fertilizer and a good CO_2 fertilizer.
Propagation: By cuttings.
Special features: Although rarely used as such, it is an ideal plant for coldwater tanks.
Water: 2-20°dH; 2-8°dCH; pH value 6-7.8; 14-28°C (57-82°F).

Ceratophyllum demersum is a fast-growing true aquatic plant, which, if kept under ideal conditions, will swamp all other plants.

Ceratophyllum demersum
LINNÉ (1753)
Hornwort

Hornwort is a fast-growing plant, which can cover the surface of an aquarium and also that of a pond within a short period of time. This makes it an ideal "starter" plant when setting up an aquarium, in order to reduce algae growth. Species from the tropics are better suited for aquatic purposes than local plants, as they are already used to the warmth. However, even local species can adapt.

Range: Worldwide.
Fertilizer: Use liquid fertilizer sparingly.
Propagation: By cuttings.
Special features: A robust coldwater species.
Water: 2-25°dH; 0-15°dCH; pH value 5.5-7.8; 4-26°C (39-79°F).

Ceratopteris thalictroides
BROGNIART (1821)
Indian fern, Water fern

An ideal floating plant for aquatic purposes; it can also be cultivated if planted.
Range: South-east Asia, northern Australia
Propagation: By cuttings
Special features: Robust and varied.
Water: 0-25°dH; 0-20°dCH; pH value 4.5-8; 20-28°C (68-82°F).

The Indian fern, Ceratopteris thalictroides, is a floating plant, but it can also be cultivated if planted into the substrate.

57

Because it is rarely imported, Crinum calamistratum *is hardly ever seen in an aquarium, although it is an ideal plant for a medium-sized tank. The larger onion plant however,* Crinum thaianum *(see photo on page 19), is a reliable plant which is often seen in larger aquariums.*

Range: Cameroon.
Fertilizer: A good substrate fertilizer, liquid fertilizer and good CO_2 fertilization.
Propagation: Vegetatively by offset bulbs, so far no other form of propagation has been successful.
Special features: Until now its natural habitat has not been discovered. The range seems to be quite limited.
Water: 2-15°dH; 2-8°dCH; pH value 6-7.5; 22-28°C (72-82°F).

Crinum calamistratum
BOGNER & HEINE (1987)

This wavy-leafed plant is rarely imported into Europe because of the political situation in its country of origin. It is quite slow-growing but is a well-suited plant for aquatics, without special requirements in respect of water conditions. The bulb of the plant has to be well anchored into the soil of the aquarium.

Crinum thaianum SCHULZE (1971)
Onion plant
Range: South Thailand.
Fertilizer: A good base fertilizer, liquid and CO_2 fertilizer.
Propagation: By offset bulbs.
Special features: There are various cultivars and naturally occurring varieties.
Water: 2-20°dH; 2-8°dCH; pH value 6-7.5; 22-28°C (72-82°F).

The shady tropical forest streams of Sri Lanka are the native habitat of Cryptocoryne beckettii. The lighting in the aquarium therefore must not be too bright.

Cryptocoryne beckettii
TRIMEN (1885)

Cryptocoryne beckettii is an aquatic plant found in bogs and moors. It adapts easily to changing water conditions and even enjoys a long life when totally submerged.

A pretty and long-lasting plant, it should be planted in the centre of the aquarium. It is a multi-coloured plant and the individual colours depend on a number of factors. The upper surfaces of the leaves are usually olive-green to brown whereas the colour of the lower surfaces range from a hint of red to purple.

The flowers always appear on the surface of the water and consist of a spathe with a single leaf. Each spathe has female and male flowering parts.

C.beckettii is a slow-growing plant and it takes several weeks before it is fully rooted in the substrate. The plant prefers a mix of sand, clay and peat as substrate. It will not tolerate a chalky soil.

Range: Sri Lanka.

Fertilizer: A good substrate and CO_2 fertilizer.

Propagation: By sideshoots.

Special features: An ideal cryptocoryne for the aquarist.

Water: 2-10°dH; 0-6°dCH; pH value 6-7.8; 22-28°C (72-82°F).

Cryptocoryne undulata
WENDT (1955)

This attractive and reliable aquatic plant is mainly used in tropical softwater aquariums. A relatively small-growing plant, it can be planted at the front as well as in the middle of the aquarium.
Range: Sri Lanka.
Fertilizer: Good base fertilizer.
Propagation: By runners.
Special features: A problem-free plant.
Water: 0-20°dH; 0-8°dCH; pH value 5-7; 20-28°C (68-82°F).

Above:
Cryptocoryne fusca *has only recently become more popular with aquarists.*

Right:
Cryptocoryne x willisii.

Cryptocoryne fusca
DE WIT (1970)

Cryptocoryne fusca is a more demanding species.
Range: Indonesia, Borneo.
Fertilizer: Good substrate fertilizer and liquid fertilizer for the water.
Propagation: By runners.
Special features: Enrich the substrate with peat and copper beech leaves to promote growth of this acid-loving plant.
Water: 0-12°dH; 0-8°dCH; pH value 5.5-7.2; 21-27°C (70-81°F).

Left:
Cryptocoryne undulata. *It is a reliable bog plant best planted in the centre of the aquarium where the lighting is not too bright.*

Cryptocoryne wendtii
DE WIT (1958)

This *Cryptocoryne* is a robust variety and is widely used in aquariums. It prefers moderate lighting.
Range: Sri Lanka.
Fertilizer: Use substrate and liquid fertilizer sparingly.
Propagation: By runners and sideshoots.
Special features: A reliable plant but some colour varieties and cultivated species are difficult to keep as aquatic plants.
Water: 0-12°dH; 0-5°dCH; pH value 5-6.8; 21-28°C (70-82°F).

Cryptocoryne x *willisii*
REITZ (1908)

A reliable and popular aquatic plant.
Range: Sri Lanka.

Fertilizer: Substrate fertilizer.
Propagation: By runners.
Special features: This plant is a hybrid of *Cryptocoryne beckettii* and *Cryptocoryne parva*.
Water: 0-15°dH; 0-8°dCH; pH value 6-7; 20-28°C (68-82°F).

Above:
Cryptocoryne wendtii.

The "Harbig" cultivar of the spade-leaf plant, Echinodorus cordifolius. This plant needs plenty of space, good lighting and, because of its fast-growing habit, plentiful fertilization. This species is best kept in open aquariums where the plants can grow out of the tank. If kept in a closed aquarium, the leaves will get "burnt". Despite its attractive foliage, owners of smaller aquariums must do without this plant.

Echinodorus cordifolius
GRISEBACH (1857)
Radicans sword, Spade-leaf plant

The majority of Amazonian sword plants are bog plants; however, they can survive being partially and sometimes even totally submerged. The spade-leaf plant belongs to this category, but as it can grow to over 1m (39in) high, the leaves will soon reach the surface of the water. Propagation is very easy as this large plant produces adventitious plantlets almost constantly if kept emersed. Propagation by seeds is difficult and this technique cannot be recommended to inexperienced aquarists.

Range: South, Central and North America.

Fertilizer: Good substrate fertilizer, liquid fertilizer for the water and CO_2 fertilizer.

Propagation: By adventitious plantlets produced when emersed.

Special features: Remove the floating leaves to prevent the plant from shedding its submerged leaves and to guarantee a long life. The plant then uses its energy to produce new leaves, which will slow down overall growth dramatically. The plant can only be kept totally submerged in very large aquariums (1m/39in or deeper). For optimum care keep spade-leaf plants in an open aquarium where they can grow up out of the tank.

Water: 2-20°dH; 2-8°dCH; pH value 6-7.5; 20-28°C (68-82°F).

Echinodorus grisebachii is a relatively large plant which needs a lot of light but has no other special requirements.

Echinodorus grisebachii
SMALL (1909)

An excellent impressive aquatic plant, which can grow to up to half a metre tall (20in), a fact which must be taken into account when setting up your aquarium.

Range: South and Central America.

Fertilizer: Good substrate fertilizer, liquid fertilizer for the water and a good CO_2 fertilizer.

Propagation: By adventitious plantlets.

Special features: *E. grisebachii* is often mistaken for other sword plants (*E. bleheri, E. gracilis, E. parviflorus*).

Water: 2-20°dH; 0-8°dCH; pH value 6-7.5; 22-28°C (72-82°F).

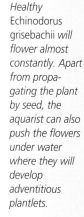

Healthy Echinodorus grisebachii will flower almost constantly. Apart from propagating the plant by seed, the aquarist can also push the flowers under water where they will develop adventitious plantlets.

Left:
Echinodorus horizontalis. *Numerous adventitious plantlets develop on the flower stems even on the water surface.*

Right:
Echinodorus osiris. *This picture shows the green-leafed wild species. The red form is more common in our aquariums.*

Echinodorus horizontalis
RATAJ (1969)

A medium-sized robust bog plant well suited for aquatic purposes.
Range: South America.
Fertilizer: Good substrate fertilizer, liquid fertilizer for the water and a good CO_2 fertilizer.
Propagation: By adventitious plantlets.
Special features: Prefers soft and slightly acidic water.
Water: 0-16°dH; 0-8°dCH; pH value 5.5-6.8; 22-28°C (72-82°F).

Echinodorus osiris
RATAJ (1970)

For a sword plant this is a relatively small species and since its discovery a few years ago it has become very popular.
Range: Southern Brazil.
Fertilizer: Intensive fertilization of all kinds.
Propagation: By adventitious plantlets.
Special features: Prefers soft slightly acidic water. Some cultivars have red leaves.
Water: 0-16°dH; 0-8°dCH; pH value 5.5-6.8; 18-25°C (64-77°F).

The pygmy chain sword plant, Echinodorus tenellus, is a popular foreground plant. It needs strong lighting for healthy growth.

Echinodorus tenellus
BUCHENAU (1868)
Pygmy chain sword plant

A popular and reliable foreground plant, which needs a lot of light to show off its grass-like appearance. Ideally you should install an additional fluorescent light tube at the front when setting up your aquarium. Provide a small-grained substrate (e.g. sand) so it can root easily.

Range: The tropics of America.

Fertilizer: Good substrate fertilizer, large amounts of liquid fertilizer in the water and a good CO_2 fertilizer.

Propagation: By adventitious plantlets.

Special features: This is a relatively small bog and shallow water variety.

Water: 0-16°dH; 0-7°dCH; pH value 6-8; 20-28°C (68-82°F).

The giant elodea, Egeria densa, is relatively easy coldwater plant, which will also adapt to the conditions of a tropical warmwater aquarium. The plant prefers high water levels.

65

Egeria densa
PLANCHON (1849)
Giant elodea

The giant elodea is much better suited to aquariums then *E. canadensis*, which was introduced to Europe and is nowadays often found in our waters.
Range: America, west Africa, Australia, New Zealand, Europe and Japan.
Fertilizer: Liquid and CO_2 fertilizer.
Propagation: By cuttings.
Special features: A good aquatic plant.
Water: 2-20°dH; 2-8°dCH; pH value 6-7.5; 10-22°C (50-72°F).

Eleocharis acicularis
ROEMER & SCHULTES (1817)
Dwarf hairgrass

A plant suitable for the foreground and middleground in heated and unheated aquariums. Plenty of light and a fine substrate are important.
Range: Worldwide.
Fertilizer: Substrate and CO_2 fertilizer.
Propagation: By adventitious plantlets.
Special features: Only experts can tell this plant apart from its many close relatives.
Water: 2-20°dH, 2-8°dCH; pH value 6-7.5; 10-28°C (50-82°F).

Left: *Dwarf hairgrass,* Eleocharis acicularis, *is an ideal foreground plant.*

Right: *The umbrella hairgrass,* Eleocharis vivipara, *is also relatively easy to look after. However, the fine stems make it look rather unattractive.*

Eleocharis vivipara
LINK (1827)
Umbrella hairgrass

The umbrella hairgrass, although a long-established aquatic plant, is not very popular and widespread because of its thin and long-winded growth.
Range: North America.
Fertilizer: Substrate and CO_2 fertilizer.
Propagation: By cuttings.
Special features: Several different species exist which are hard to distinguish.
Water: 2-20°dH; 0-8°dCH; pH value 6-7.5; 8-26°C (46-79°F).

Hemianthus micranthemoides
NUTTAL (1817)

This plant needs plenty of light but is otherwise easy to cultivate.
Range: North America.
Fertilizer: Very undemanding.
Propagation: By cuttings.
Special features: Needs plenty of light.
Water: 2-20°dH; 0-8°dCH; pH value 6-7.5; 20-28°C (68-82°F).

Hottonia palustris
LINNÉ (1753)
Water violet

The water violet is, like many aquatic plants, actually a bog plant, which can survive totally submerged provided it gets sufficient light and fertilizer.
Range: Europe and North Asia.
Fertilizer: Good substrate fertilizer, liquid fertilizer and a good CO_2 fertilizer.
Propagation: By cuttings.
Special features: A rare native bog plant. Most plants available from aquatic shops are cultivated varieties, which do not always adapt easily to life under water. Ideally keep the plant only partially submerged to begin with and only lower it further into the water once the tell-tale differently shaped underwater leaves start to form. This is the only way *H. palustris* will adapt to being totally submerged.
Water: 2-20°dH; 0-8°dCH; pH value 6-7.5; 4-25°C (39-77°F).

Hemianthus micranthemoides can be planted either as a foreground plant or in the middle of the tank as long as it is cut back regularly. It requires a lot of light.

67

Species

Hottonia palustris *is a European bog plant, which is now rarely seen in our aquariums. It needs plenty of light and fertilizer to survive submerged.*

Hydrocotyle verticillata *is a demanding aquatic plant and will only thrive in an aquarium as long as it gets plenty of light and fertilizer.*

Hydrocotyle verticillata
THUNBERG (1798)
Pennywort

The unusually shaped leaves makes pennyworts popular aquatic plants, but they are very demanding in respect of light and fertilization. It is also important to maintain good water quality.

Range: South and North America.
Fertilizer: Good substrate, liquid and CO_2 fertilizer.
Propagation: By cuttings.
Special features: Several varieties with different flower stems are known.
Water: 2-20°dH; 0-8°dCH; pH value 6-7.3; 15-25°C (59-77°F).

Hygrophila corymbosa
LINDAU (1895)
Giant hygrophila

An ideal aquatic plant, although very tall-growing; it needs to be cut back regularly.
Range: South-east Asia.
Fertilizer: Liquid fertilizer in the water and a good CO_2 fertilizer.
Propagation: By cuttings.
Special features: Various forms with different leaves and colours are available.
Water: 2-20°dH; 0-8°dCH; pH value 5-7.8; 20-30°C (68-86°F).

Hygrophila difformis
BLUME (1826)
Water wisteria

A reliable aquatic plant, and hardly any aquarium is complete without it. It is easy-growing, robust and a popular species.
Range: South-east Asia.
Fertilizer: Liquid fertilizer in the water and a good CO_2 fertilizer.
Propagation: By cuttings.
Special features: Many shapes and forms.
Water: 0-20°dH; 0-8°dCH; pH value 5-7; 21-30°C (70-86°F).

Above left:
Hygrophila corymbosa *is a robust species.*

Above right:
Hygrophila difformis.

69

The dwarf hygrophila, Hygrophila polysperma, is a good aquatic plant, although with insufficient lighting it will produce long internodes, which make it look less attractive than its relatives.

Hygrophila polysperma
ANDERSON (1867)
Dwarf hygrophila

Another robust and reliable aquatic plant; however, compared to other hygrophilas, it has less conspicuous leaves and is therefore not as popular as its relatives.

Range: India.

Fertilizer: Liquid fertilizer in the water and CO_2 fertilizer.

Propagation: By cuttings.

Special features: Its growth depends on the intensity of light it experiences.

Water: 0-20°dH; 0-8°dCH; pH value 5-8; 10-26°C (50-79°F).

Like all Hygrophila species, some of the dwarf hygrophila cultivars have coloured leaves or leaf veins caused by the action of viruses. These forms are generally much more delicate than the wild types.

Lilaeopsis brasiliensis *makes an ideal foreground plant, but it needs plenty of light so that it can form a nice carpet.*

Below:
Limnophila hete-rophylla.

Lilaeopsis brasiliensis
AFFOLTER (1985)

An ideal foreground plant, which requires bright lighting for optimum growth.

Range: South America (another species comes from New Zealand, but this has not been introduced to aquatics).

Fertilizer: Good substrate fertilizer, liquid fertilizer in the water and a good CO_2 fertilizer.

Propagation: By runners.

Special features: This species is known as *Lilaeopsis novaezelandiae* in aquatic circles; this latter species does actually exist but it has not yet been imported for aquarium use.

Water: 2-25°dH; 0-10°dCH; pH value 5.5-7.2; 22-28°C (72-82°F).

71

Like many other stem plants, Limnophila heterophylla produces fine roots from the nodes on the stem so new cuttings can root easily.

Ludwigia repens has been crossed with many other Ludwigia, which has produced many attractive forms with distinctively coloured leaves.

Limnophila heterophylla
BENTHAM (1835)

Limnophilas are very popular aquatic plants because of their finely structured leaves. They do not require much care and are often used as background plants or for the central area of the aquarium.

Range: Asia, South-east Asia.

Fertilizer: Plenty of liquid fertilizer in the water and good CO_2 fertilizer.

Propagation: By cuttings.

Special features: The different varieties of *Limnophila* can only be identified by their flowers.

Water: 2-20°dH; 2-8°dCH; pH value 6-7.5; 20-28°C (68-82°F).

Ludwigia repens
FORSTER (1771)

Ludwigia repens is a popular aquatic plant because of its green stems and the numerous varieties that are available. Bright lighting will prevent the stems growing tall and the plant will stay compact and bushy. Don't pinch out the tips of the stems too often as this will make them thin and brittle.

Range: North and Central America.

Fertilizer: Liquid fertilizer in the water and plenty of CO_2 fertilizer.

Propagation: By cuttings.

Special features: This plant is a hybrid of *Ludwigia arcuata* and *L. palustris*.

Water: 2-20°dH; 2-8°dCH; pH value 6-7.5; 20-28°C (68-82°F).

The green Ludwigia repens is not as eye-catching in colour as its red-coloured relatives. Despite this, it is a very good aquatic plant and easy to look after.

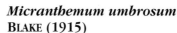

Micranthemum umbrosum
BLAKE (1915)

This bog plant can survive being fully submerged provided sufficient light and fertilizer is provided. Although its stems have to be trimmed back frequently, the plant has established itself as a reliable foreground plant. Trimming is not difficult as the whole plant can simply be cut and it will happily shoot up again.

Range: North America.

Fertilizer: Liquid fertilizer in the water and CO_2 fertilizer.

Propagation: By cuttings.

Special features: Although it is naturally a coldwater plant, it will adapt to conditions in an aquarium.

Water: 2-20°dH; 0-8°dCH; pH value 6-7.5; 10-24°C (50-75°F).

Micranthemum umbrosum is one of the few stem plants that can be planted in the foreground. Long stems are simply cut back so the plant produces new growth and this strengthens the root system.

73

The Java fern, Microsorum pteropus, *can be used to cover decorations. This versatile plant is ideal for concealing cork backing on the tank.*

The spores underneath the leaves hardly ever mature under aquarium conditions.

Microsorum pteropus
CHING (1933)
Java fern

The interesting "Windelov" cultivar is no more difficult to cultivate than the wild Java fern.

The Java fern is one of the most versatile of all aquatic plants. As it needs relatively little light, it is often used to cover decorations in the tank such as bogwood and rocks, where it can still compete against taller plants in shaded areas. However, the Java fern will not tolerate very hard water.

Range: Tropical Asia.
Fertilizer: No fertilizer needed.
Propagation: By runners; spores form on the back of the leaves but they hardly ever mature on aquatic plants.

Special features: A robust plant, a new interesting cultivar "Windelov" has recently been introduced.

Water: 2-18°dH; 2-8°dCH; pH value 6-8; 20-28°C (68-82°F).

Myriophyllum aquaticum *and other members of its family are reliable aquatic plants, but they all require plenty of light and mineral fertilizer.*

Myriophyllum aquaticum
Verdcourt (1973)
Parrot's feather, Diamond milfoil

Parrot's feather is a demanding but, because of its leaves, a very popular aquatic plant. Bright lighting is essential to encourage the plant to stay compact, and only in this shape is it really attractive. Lack of iron and manganese fertilizer will also be detrimental to the plant's health. The stems grow quickly into long garlands. Before taking cuttings from only the strongest shoots, allow the plant to grow on the surface of the water for quite some time, but ensure that the plants underneath are not overshadowed. Cuttings taken from strong stems root easily and are well suited to build up a stock of plants. As with all stem plants, parrot's feather is best planted in a group where it makes a beautiful contrast to plants with different leaf structures and thus enhances the overall appearance of the aquarium. Varieties with red leaves are quite difficult and more suitable for specialists.

Range: South America.

Fertilizer: Liquid fertilizer in the water and a good CO_2 fertilizer.

Propagation: By cuttings.

Special features: This plant has been spread by human intervention and now spreads vegetatively.

Water: 2-20°dH; 2-8°dCH; pH value 5.5-8; 10-28°C (50-82°F).

Nymphaea lotus *grows relatively well submerged and it forms interesting leaves below and above water level.*
Photo: Dr. Jürgen Schmidt.

Right: The crystalwort, Riccia fluitans, is actually a floating plant, which is usually found just below the water surface. If tied to rocks, it will grow on the floor of the aquarium where it produces a lawn of foliage.

Nymphaea lotus
LINNÉ (1753)
Lotus lily, Egyptian white waterlily

The lotus lily is generally used in aquariums as an underwater plant. Only rarely is it found in high or open aquariums, where it will grow floating leaves and also flower. Plenty of light and fertilizer and the removal of floating leaves will force the plant to stay submerged.

Range: Worldwide except in Asia.

Fertilizer: Good substrate fertilizer, liquid fertilizer and a good CO_2 fertilizer.

Propagation: By runners.

Special features: Numerous varieties with different leaf shapes and colours.

Water: 2-30°dH; 0-8°dCH; pH value 5.5-8; 20-30°C (68-86°F).

Riccia fluitans
LINNÉ (1753)
Crystalwort

A versatile plant used either floating or as ground cover. Ideal spawning surface.
Range: Worldwide.
Fertilizer: No fertilizer necessary.
Propagation: By splitting the plant.
Special features: Any movement on the water surface should be avoided.
Water: 2-25°dH; 0-10°dCH; pH value 5-8; 18-27°C (64-81°F).

Rotala macrandra
KOEHNE (1880)
Giant red rotala

This is an exceptionally attractive but demanding aquatic plant, and although it requires a lot of care and attention, one cannot imagine an aquarium without it. The stems which are available from aquatic shops are mostly cultivated in bog conditions, which can make them quite difficult to adapt to underwater conditions. The submerged plants produce completely different and, unfortunately, much less attractive leaves, which are small with only a hint of red.
Range: Southern India.
Fertilizer: Liquid fertilizer in the water and a good CO_2 fertilizer.
Propagation: Cuttings.
Special features: Only with intensive lighting and fertilization with iron will the plant keep its vibrant red leaves. Related species are not as demanding and easier to maintain.
Water: 2-18°dH; 0-6°dCH; pH value 5.5-7; 22-28°C (72-82°F).

The giant red rotala, Rotala macrandra, is an attractive but very demanding aquatic plant. It will only retain its red leaves under bright light and with the right amounts of iron-rich fertilizer.

Utricularia gibba LINNÉ (1753)
Humped bladderwort

A floating plant, which easily adapts to conditions in an aquarium.
Range: Worldwide; native in many parts of Europe.
Fertilizer: No fertilizer necessary; small "live food", such as larvae, beneficial.
Propagation: By cuttings.
Special features: It is a carnivorous plant.
Water: 2-20°dH; 0-5°dCH; pH value 5.5-7.5; 4-27°C (39-81°F).

Although the giant sagittaria, Sagittaria platyphylla, prefers cooler water temperatures, it does adapt well to the conditions in a tropical aquarium.

Utricularia gibba is a carnivorous plant; it grows well in aquariums.

Sagittaria platyphylla
SMITH (1894)
Giant sagittaria

Although sagittaria are reliable and good aquatic plants, they are hardly ever grown now in aquariums. They may have declined in popularity because of the faster-growing *Vallisneria* species, which are easier to keep and have similar leaves.
Range: North and Central America.
Fertilizer: Good substrate fertilizer, liquid fertilizer in the water and a good CO_2 fertilizer.
Propagation: By runners.
Special features: The plant can also be grown by a garden pond, where it is more at home than in an aquarium.
Water: 2-20°dH; 2-8°dCH; pH value 6-7.5; 18-28°C (64-82°F).

The long leaves of the straight vallisneria, Vallisneria spiralis, *lie on the surface of the water in a shallow tank and overshadow other plants.*

The Java moss, Vesicularia dubyana, *is a particularly robust aquatic plant.*

Vallisneria spiralis
LINNÉ (1753)
Straight vallisneria, Tape grass

Straight vallisneria is one of the ideal aquatic plants. It adapts to conditions in an aquarium without any problems and propagates quickly by producing runners. However, the runners need to be frequently removed and transplanted.
Range: Europe and South-west Asia.
Fertilizer: Good substrate fertilizer and liquid fertilizer in the water as well as a good CO_2 fertilizer.
Propagation: By runners.
Special features: A plant that is easy to care for and easily propagated.
Water: 4-26°dH; 2-10°dCH; pH value 6-8; 12-30°C (54-86°F).

Vesicularia dubyana
BROTHERUS (1908)
Java moss

Java moss is completely undemanding and will continue to grow without significant light and thus can be grown amongst large plants. The moss also provides good cover for decorations but it will not tolerate algae and mulm – organic debris – in the aquarium.
Range: South-east Asia.
Fertilizer: No fertilizer necessary.
Propagation: By cuttings.
Special features: Java moss is an ideal spawning medium for fish.
Water: 2-28°dH; 2-10°dCH; pH value 4.5-8.2; 12-30°C (54-86°F).

For further information
about the full Interpet range of
aquatic and pet titles, please
write to:
Interpet Publishing,
Vincent Lane,
Dorking,
Surrey,
RH4 3YX